Mix and Change

**Written by
Cheryl Jakab**

Contents

Rigby®

Chapter Snapshots

"Learn about science with
Crystal and Luis."

1 Mix and Unmix

Meet young chemists Crystal and Luis. They've been invited to visit Dr. Argon's chemistry laboratory. Today should be an exciting day.

I can't believe we're in a real laboratory, Luis. We'll need these safety goggles and gloves today.

Mixing

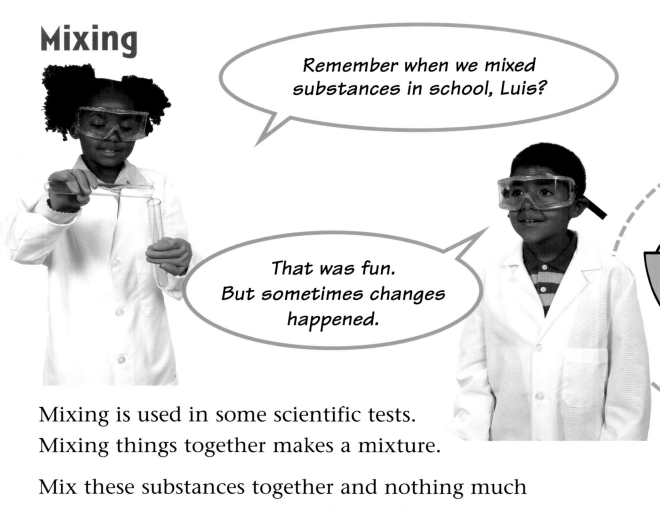

Remember when we mixed substances in school, Luis?

That was fun. But sometimes changes happened.

Mixing is used in some scientific tests. Mixing things together makes a mixture.

Mix these substances together and nothing much happens to the mixture. No chemical reaction happens.

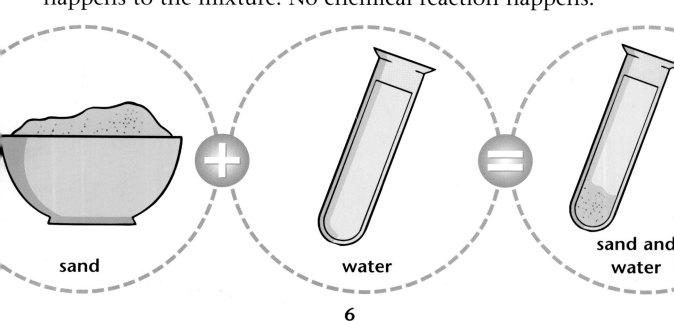

sand + water = sand and water

But mix these substances together and something changes. A chemical reaction happens!

Question: What is happening to this mixture? Turn to page 31 to find out.

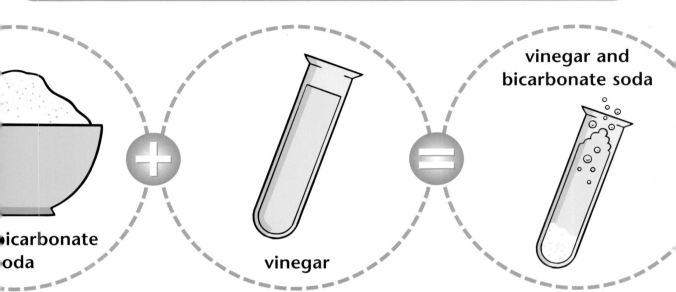

bicarbonate soda

vinegar

vinegar and bicarbonate soda

Mixtures to Eat!

Chefs are constantly developing new mixtures. These mixtures are called recipes. Chefs use different mixtures to make various cakes. Each different cake is made up of a different mixture.

"Unmixing" Mixtures

Mixtures are everywhere. Just about everything around you is made up of mixtures. Rocks, your food—even you—are made up of mixtures.

Scientists sometimes separate mixtures so that they can get a substance from the mixture.

Colorful Mixtures

Artists mix different substances together to get different colored paints. In ancient times, paints were made by crushing colored rocks and then mixing them with water, oil, honey, or other liquids.

Salt and water are separated by evaporating the water. Heat is used to evaporate the water and just the salt is left.

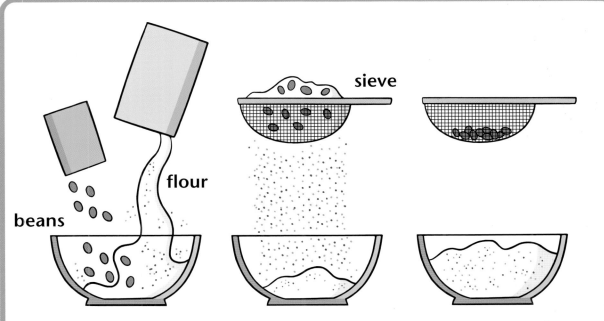

Flour and beans are separated by a sieve. The flour falls through the holes, leaving the beans in the sieve.

2 Alchemists— Yesterday's Chemists?

In school, Crystal and Luis read about alchemists. Alchemists lived long ago. They wanted to change metals into precious gold by melting and mixing them. Modern chemists know this is something that cannot be done.

Alchemists' Secrets

Alchemists thought they were going to discover how to make gold! Because of this, they didn't want anyone else to know what they were doing. So they made up secret symbols for the substances they used.

| gold | silver | copper | iron | lead | water |

Question: What were alchemists trying to do? Turn to page 31 to find out.

Burning Questions

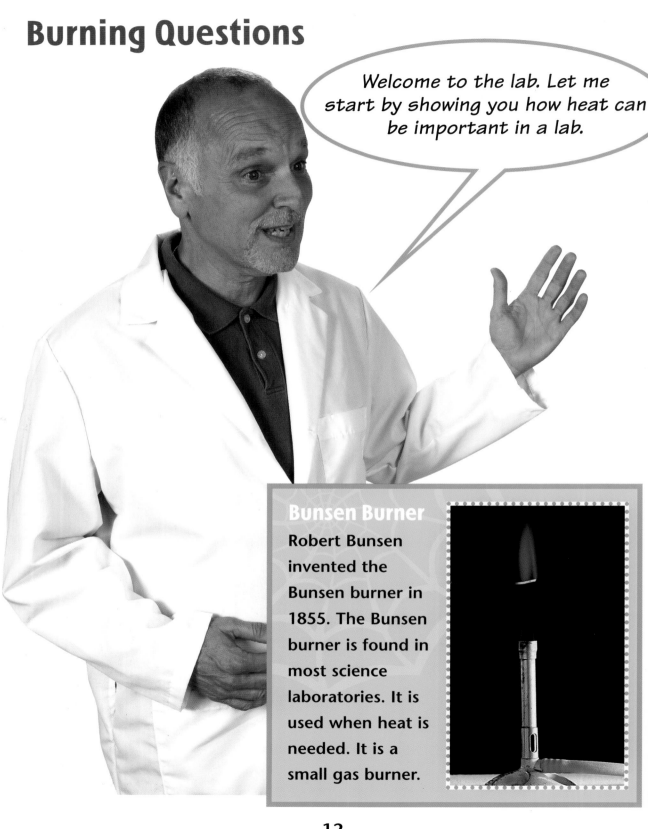

Welcome to the lab. Let me start by showing you how heat can be important in a lab.

Bunsen Burner

Robert Bunsen invented the Bunsen burner in 1855. The Bunsen burner is found in most science laboratories. It is used when heat is needed. It is a small gas burner.

Yes! Show us what you mean!

Heating can be a scientific test. Heating sometimes makes new substances. Different substances have different colored flames. Scientists know what is being heated by looking at the color of the flames.

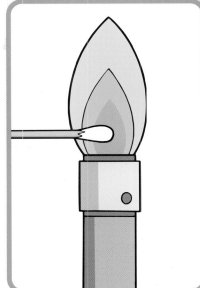

This flame is burning yellow. Sodium is a substance that burns with a yellow flame.

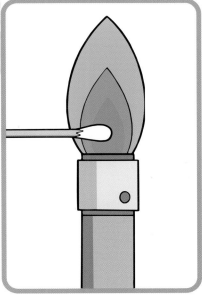

This flame is burning green. Boric acid is a substance that burns with a green flame.

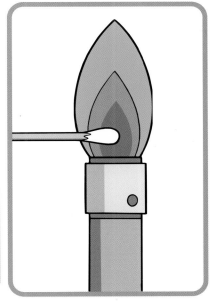

This flame is burning orange. Salt is a substance that burns with an orange flame.

Experimenting with Substances

Experimenting can be fun, as long as safety rules are always followed. Dr. Argon is writing a secret message with invisible ink. Invisible ink is a special substance.

Are you using lemon juice?

No, this invisible ink is made from sugar in water. Invisible ink can be made with any clear liquid that changes color when heated.

Invisible Inks

Substances that are clear or pale are hard to see when put on paper. A good invisible ink burns and changes color to black or brown when heated. Remember that an adult should be present whenever heat is used to create changes.

This invisible ink is a brownish colour when heated.

Crystal and Luis are mixing up an interesting mixture they call "goo!" Goo is a substance that is sometimes a solid and sometimes a liquid.

Wonderful! Squeeze this and it feels solid.

Stop squeezing and it is liquid.

Making Goo

Not quite solid, but not quite liquid! It's goo!

 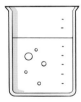 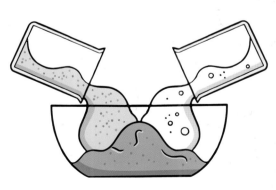

1/4 cup water

3/4 teaspoon borax laundry detergent

10 drops food colouring

2 tablespoons white glue

2 tablespoons water

2 tablespoons borax mixture

"Goo!"

3 Dr. Argon in the Lab

The Kitchen Laboratory

Spending the morning mixing and creating substances can make you hungry. Now it's time for lunch in another laboratory. This laboratory is called the kitchen!

SHOPPING
LIST

Question: What changes are happening in this kitchen laboratory? Turn to page 31 to find out.

The Scientist's Workroom

Dr. Argon demonstrates how to use equipment in the laboratory. Can you name the equipment? (Hint: Use the key provided.)

Tell us about the equipment in your laboratory.

Each piece of equipment has a special job.

Key

 Bunsen burner

 flask

 scales

 pipettes

 chemicals

 warning signs

 burette

test tube rack
and test tubes

Chemicals

In the scientist's lab, there is special equipment for studying chemicals.

The whole world is made of chemicals. Every item is made up of chemicals.

Question: Which of the following are made up of chemicals? Turn to page 31 to find out.

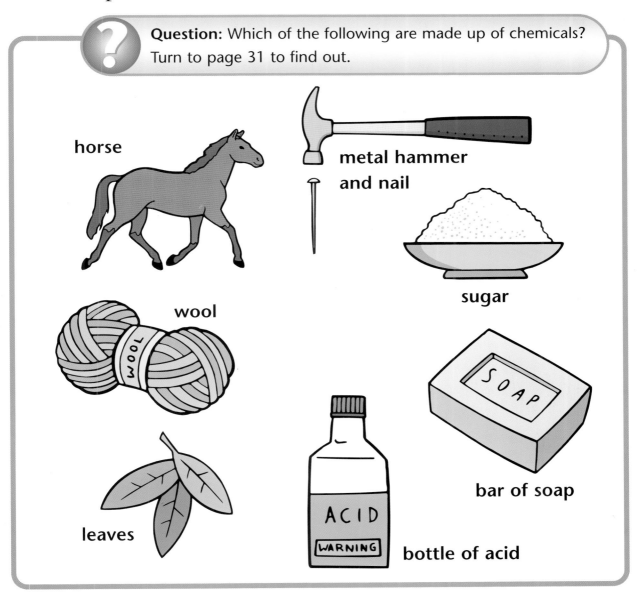

horse

metal hammer and nail

sugar

wool

bar of soap

leaves

bottle of acid

What Are Chemicals?

Chemical is another word for a substance. Chemicals are not just the chemicals that are in bottles at a scientist's laboratory. Chemicals make up all the substances around us.

4 Metals

Many metals are chemical elements. This means they can't be broken down into simpler substances.

I received a silver bracelet for my birthday. Silver is a metal.

The metal I want to know most about is gold!

Amazing Gold

Gold is very malleable. This means it can be easily made into different shapes. Gold is so malleable that one ounce can be made into a thread 50 miles long!

These items are all metal.
Use the key to learn about
the metals here.

Metal Key
1 **Copper:** soft reddish metal
2 **Stainless steel:** does not rust
3 **Aluminum:** light, white metal used in cans
4 **Lead:** very heavy, soft metal
5 **Silver:** shiny metal used to make jewelry
6 **Iron:** strong, soft, easy to work metal that rusts

What Are Metals?

Most metals are hard and shiny. They usually "clang" when hit by something hard. Metals can be made into almost any shape.

Question: Which of the following are metals? Turn to page 31 to find out.

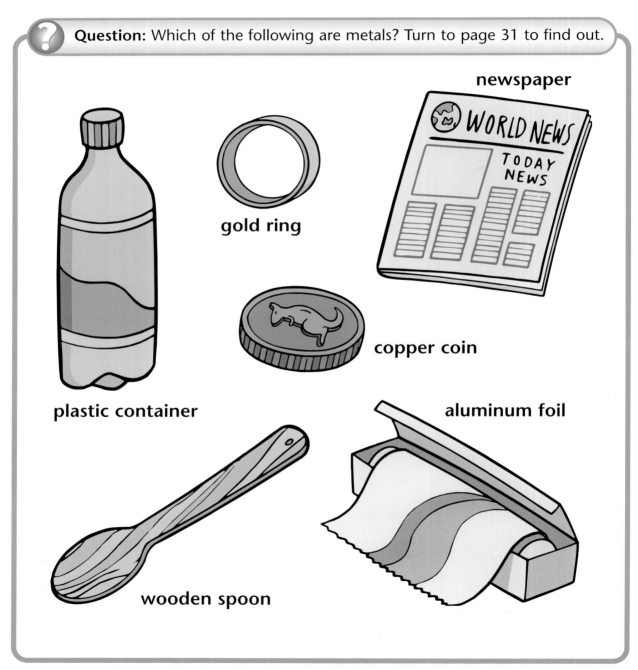

newspaper

gold ring

copper coin

plastic container

aluminum foil

wooden spoon

What else is copper used for?

Copper can be combined with zinc or tin to make brass or bronze.

We have candleholders made of brass at home.

Copper

Copper is used many places in the home. It conducts electricity, so it is used for electrical wiring. Copper pots and pans heat evenly, so they are good for cooking. Water pipes are often made of copper, because copper doesn't corrode, or wear away, easily. Copper also stops certain bacteria from growing in water.

5 Dr. Argon and Science

Same and Different

Dr. Argon explains how scientists explore different materials. This way they can learn about a material's properties and are able to classify it.

Crystal and Luis explore whether some materials will float.

What Is the Same about Oil, Water, and Honey?

Oil, water, and honey are all liquids. They can be poured. But oil, water, and honey are also quite different from each other. They are all different colours. Honey is the thickest of these liquids.

 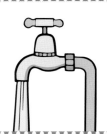 

Observing and Describing

Scientists observe and describe the properties of materials. They then group materials with similar properties. Some groups of materials include powders, crystals, metals, liquids, and gases.

Plastics

Plastics are synthetic materials. The word plastic means 'to shape.' Heating easily shapes plastics.

plastic fork and spoon

plastic bowl

 Question: Why can't plastic dishes be used in the oven? Turn to page 31 to find out.

Investigating Properties

We can ask questions to help us explore and learn about all these materials.

Is it a solid, liquid, or a gas?

What does it look like?

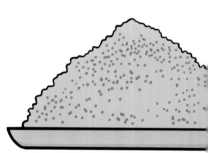

How does it feel to touch?

Does it bend?

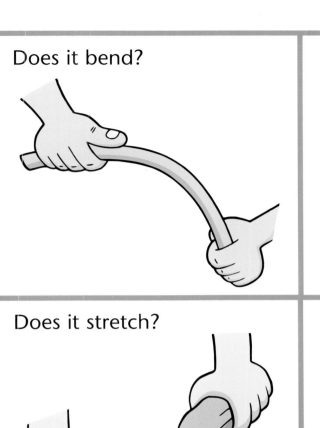

Is it heavy for its size?

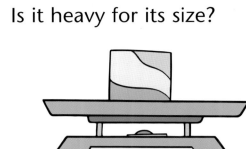

Does it stretch?

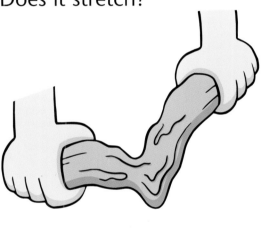

Does it float?

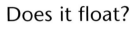
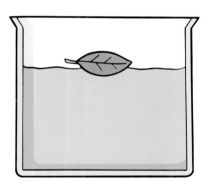

How hard is it?

How does it react when mixed?

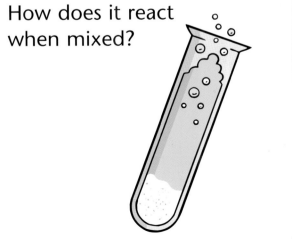

Good-bye, Dr. Argon!

My job as a chemist is to study the properties of materials. I ask questions and then do tests to find the answers. I'm always happy to have visitors in my lab. Thank you for coming.

Good-bye! And thank you for letting us visit!

Questions and Answers

PAGE 7

Question: What is happening to this mixture?

Answer: The mixture is bubbling. The bubbles are carbon dioxide.

PAGE 11

Question: What were alchemists trying to do?

Answer: They were trying to change metals into gold, by melting and mixing the metals.

PAGES 16/17

Question: What changes are happening in this kitchen laboratory?

Answer: Many changes are happening. **Toaster:** the bread is being heated. **Saucepan:** the water is being heated. **Blender:** the pieces of food are being mixed together. **Sink:** the detergent is being mixed with water. Bubbles are made.

PAGE 21

Question: Which of the following are chemicals?

Answer: All of the items are made up of chemicals.

PAGE 24

Question: Which of the following are metals?

Answer: The gold ring, copper coin, and aluminum foil are all metals.

PAGE 27

Question: Why can't plastic dishes be used in the oven?

Answer: Heating softens plastics, so plastic dishes melt in the oven.

Index

Bookweb Links

Read more books at Grade 3 in Bookweb and Bookweb Plus about observing, changing, and sorting materials:

Silk, Satins, or Synthetics — Non Fiction

Let's Collect That! — Non Fiction

In the Kitchen — Non Fiction

Sensational! — Non Fiction

The Perfect Lawn — Fiction

Hugo and Spot — Fiction

Key to Bookweb Fact Boxes
- ■ Arts
- ■ Health
- ■ Science
- ■ Social Studies
- ■ Technology